Have you ever wondered about magnets?

A magnet contains a force that attracts certain metals, like iron.

Long ago, people discovered that some metal objects would stick to a special rock.

This rock is called lodestone.

Today, people make their own magnets.

horseshoe
magnet

block
magnets

Magnets come in all shapes and sizes.

U-shaped magnet

bar magnet

disk magnets

rod magnets

N

Every magnet has a north pole and a south pole.

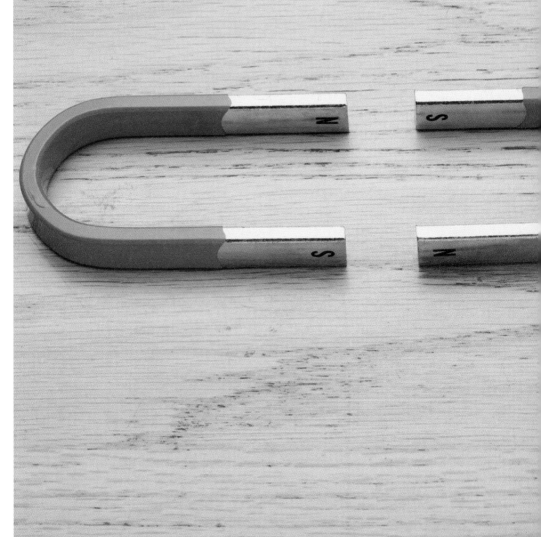

A magnet is strongest at its poles.

A needle in a compass is a magnet.

It always points to the north pole of Earth.

See how these iron filings gather around this magnet?

This is called the magnetic field.

Which of these things do you think will stick to a magnet?

These paper clips will stick to a magnet.

So will these bells!

Magnets come in all shapes and sizes.

Look how
much
this giant
magnet
can hold!